IS THIS WHAT WE EXPECTED?

**Exploding
assumptions
about
women's
lives
after 60**

GW00685394

IDA • 1

FOREWORD

The Ida Project is the idea of three friends – Belinda Budge, Ann Treneman and Vicky Wilson. It came about when we realised that we had been talking a lot recently about the new discoveries and challenges we were facing, and wondered if we could involve other women over 60 in a creative conversation about this stage of our lives.

The three of us met back in 1986 on a Women's Studies MA course at the University of Kent and subsequently set up a feminist publishing company, Scarlet Press. Our aim then was to provoke debate and explore issues we felt had been underrepresented, and one of our series, the *Lesbians Talk Issues* pamphlets, did just that. Recently digitised by the Bishopsgate Institute library in London, the series was one of our inspirations.

Our other inspiration was New York feminist and activist artist Ida Applebroog, who in the late 1970s circulated her work by sending self-published pamphlets to friends through the post. Our initial call-out for people to join the Ida Project therefore came in the form of a postcard, and this pamphlet is a further homage to the idea that not everything needs to be online.

The pages that follow contain the responses we received to our invitation to join a 'creative conversation about women's lives from their 60s to their 90s'. The postcards were sent only to friends (or friends of friends) so we make no claim that the participants are in any way representative of the wider female population (and indeed they are not). However, their responses do embody a range of experiences, perspectives and attitudes that we found by turns moving, provocative, challenging and inspiring. It was more than we expected – and we feel that collectively their words explode some of the pernicious assumptions about older women's lives. We thank everyone who responded to our invitation.

We hope that after this small start, the conversation and range of participants will grow. Contributors to the Ida Project have suggested many directions in which the conversation could be taken forward and we are excited at the idea of being able to pursue as many of these as possible.

Please get in touch if you would like to join us and we will continue to keep all our participants informed about whatever happens next.

Belinda, Ann and Vicky
info@theidaproject.com

CONTENTS

FRANCES KNIGHT HOW OLD ARE YOU?

How old are you? Throughout my life I have found this an awkward question – one which I am prone to dodge, either by outright lying or changing the subject. When I do reply, the figure I give seems to mean something to the person who asked me – but what exactly does the number of earth's revolutions around the sun really signify, and how does it define me? Is it how I am, or who I am?

The words 'I am' are often used to define one's identity or current state. But how many other identity traits, like age, change on the stroke of midnight every year? No wonder we need cake and/or champagne to help us through this annual metamorphosis.

Some languages, like French or Italian, use 'I have' (as in *j'ai [xx] ans / ho [xx] anni*). This puts the emphasis on time as something we have lived through. Rather than being a number that defines us, we have these years and they add to the sum of our experience.

This may be fanciful and just a product of random linguistic history. However, for me anything that destabilises this seemingly innocuous question is worth exploring.

MANDY BUDGE

I remember how impactful Dale Spender's *Man Made Language* was in the early 1980s when I was starting out as a teacher. It was radical and those of us working in primary schools started reading stories with all animals as SHE. This was powerful and made a ripple. I hope the way we opened up language to give girls a place within it opened up opportunities as well. And I think we need to revolutionise language in a similar way to deal with age.

We so easily slip into the habit of counting our years away, saying we can't believe we are nearly 70, or 80, or 90. It's as if our expectations of these ages are so low, and we are surprised to find we are still getting some pleasure from life, still able to function. So many terms associated with older women have negative connotations (the Collins dictionary defines calling someone an old woman as being critical of them for being overanxious) – not to mention the crones, hags, and wizened witches of fairytales.

For our own sakes and for the way the rest of society perceives us, we need to explode the assumptions embedded in our language so we can think of ageing as positive and express this in the way we talk about it.

BRIDGET FARRANDS

First of all, I was totally surprised that I could ever even *be* 60. It seemed to be such an old age, and one that could never apply to me.

For my 60th birthday, my husband organised a surprise women-only party. There in front of me – once I got over the surprise of finding friends it usually took me weeks to arrange to see – were about 40 women of all shapes, sizes, energy levels and wrinkliness, all meeting each other, laughing, chatting and generally creating an uproar, all having huge fun celebrating my birthday. I had to admit that being 60 was the best age (after being 55). It was the start of my experience that age is what I make it, not what other people tell me.

Now I celebrate every birthday as just a number and use my own feelings as the guide to getting older – not what society tells me. My confidence in who I am as an older woman – now in her 70s – is growing, alongside the wrinkles. So thank you, friends!

KATHERINE UKLEJA
HERSELF SURPRISED

Decades ago, Joyce Cary's *Herself Surprised* was on my sixth-form reading list, one of a number of books on the theme of 'a dedicated life'. We are talking the Antipodes in the late 1960s here, so all the books were about men – with the exception of *The Lady with the Lamp*, of course, the subtext being that any girl still at school should follow the example of Florence Nightingale.

Instead, I chose Cary's Gulley Jimson, a painter of considerable talent and a dissolute, womanising scoundrel. He was certainly dedicated to his art, not letting any social or moral mores get in the way. Despite his significant shortcomings, he held appeal for my teenage self, tickling my rebellious streak and my growing resistance to a male-defined femininity.

Now in my 70s, I find myself surprised to be still in a small pool of limelight – still teaching, still followed by thousands on Facebook, still invited to speak at conferences. I function as an elder in a global tribe of fringe-dwellers in the field of complementary therapy, or, as I prefer it, alternative medicine.

Of course, I am invisible to the male gaze – not that turning heads was ever a big feature of my life. But my voice is still heard, and my voice still diverges from the mainstream.

MARIE MULVEY-ROBERTS
60 IS THE NEW 40

So how *has* the 60s turned out? Soon future generations will not have the luxury of asking, which one?

Being a child of the 60s (and a baby of the 50s), it is sobering for me to reflect, 60 years on, on what might have been and to wonder where all that hedonism went. Back then, people in their 60s seemed positively geriatric, as we probably still do to the young. As for me, I don't feel that much has changed since I moved into adulthood – except that this is definitely my happiest decade.

When I turned 50, I decided to mark it by doing something I had never done before – a one-handed handstand! It got me wondering then how I could mark the end of that decade with something even more extraordinary. But on reaching 60, I discovered that I did not have the slightest inclination to do anything so strenuous – not because I was physically incapable, but because I simply couldn't be bothered – and what a relief that felt!

I am still doing the same job I started 35 years ago. I became a Professor in my 60s – the fulfilment of a dream. I am as productive and busy as ever – though I feel less pressurised these days, despite the challenges facing us academics who have to balance our teaching with administration and research.

I have made a new departure in my 60s into film-making, designing websites, have started playing the pipe organ again and got married for the first and only time. Much of my life is taken up in helping my husband to look after a two-acre woodland garden on the side of a valley and to maintain a very old property, which is all good exercise.

We took on this place on in our 60s and went in the opposite direction to downsizing. That defiance has marked my sixth decade. Apart from tinges of baby-boomer guilt, life is good – and yes, better than it was in the other 60s!

VICKY WILSON 65 IS THE NEW 25

From the perspective of 25-year-old me, the lives of women over 60 seemed fixed and unchangeable, with thoughts and conversation mired in the trivia of the everyday. So I didn't expect my own 60s to feel more like my 20s – a time of rapid change and fluctuating emotions – after the more stable period of my 40s and 50s. There seems to be no roadmap for this new landscape – though at least now I know myself better.

After living in the same house in the same small seaside town for 22 years, my partner and I – more or less on the spur of the moment – moved to a city to be closer to our family. I've loved exploring new streets and discovering new walks, listening to more live music, watching more cinema, experiencing more life going on around us. But I have no illusions that this will be the last or even second-, third-, or fourth-to-last place I live. It seems that at this age, none of us can predict what we might be doing in ten, five or even a year's time.

This sense of returning to the lifestyle of my younger self pops up in other ways. In my 20s and early 30s, most of my friends seemed to be frequently changing partners, jobs and homes, hedonistically enjoying whatever was available, as well as fighting the vicious homophobia of Section 28, battling misogyny across numerous fronts, and watching loved ones die too young from AIDS. It was in turns exhilarating and intensely painful.

I certainly didn't expect the same degree of fluidity in our lives now, as friends negotiate new roles and identities – whether as grandparents, retirees, or pursuing dreams as writers, dancers and designers –. and/or fall sick, are widowed or take on roles of full-time carers (or any combination of the above). Along with the heartache, some of the hedonism has returned too, as those of us who still can determine to enjoy the time we have left.

I also didn't expect us to find ourselves fighting battles I thought were already won – especially a toxic misogyny that seems to have swelled into an evangelical movement. I lived through the Thatcher years but still didn't foresee the extent of the political poison more recent Conservative governments have delivered: the removal of our rights as European citizens, the wholesale impoverishment of the NHS (particularly worrying for us older people), the demonisation of refugees, the staggering increase in inequality, not to mention the unchecked destruction of the planet… I feel privileged to have been protected from some of this by my whiteness and relative wealth (as part of a generation for whom home ownership was affordable and with an income protected by a pension triple lock), but also increasingly angry.

Twenty-five-year-old me would have been surprised at this depth of feeling, as well as at the openness and passion of my 60+ contemporaries. We still have a lot to offer – so let's make sure we stay visible and that our different voices can still be heard.

ROSA WOOLF AINLEY

But how much has it really turned out differently from what I expected? I always trotted out that line about every generation having to remake everything in their own way, but maybe I didn't really believe it would apply to our generation, because things were on the move, changing for the better – or that's how it seemed at some point, in relation to equalities and diversity.

Not anymore. Among too many examples to list are the continuing existence of the gender pay gap; horrific systemic racism within education and policing; the increase in food/heat/bed poverty (even necessitating new terminology); and the attitudes to social housing that led to the bedroom tax, which disgusted me so much I wrote a novel about it.

As a writer, I'm all ears for new words, new forms, new uses, and want language to be always in process. Otherwise we're really in trouble. But while I'm delighted to play with it on the page, speaking it takes longer to sound right somehow, as though I'm using someone else's script, and in a way I suppose I am.

Or I'm using someone else's platform, going back to whether to shift from emoticon to emoji or, more recently, whether I follow on to TikTok and X (that's an easy no for me – never bothered much with formerly Twitter either). There's a sense all round that this probably isn't for me.

New technologies had – and still have – immense capacity to even up disparities. And yet the question remains, how do we keep up with the new, and do we want to? If we do want to, is that ok, or should we keep to our own, known ideas and ways of being?

I recently learned to do some AR (augmented reality) programming and coding. I was keen to learn about the possibilities and saw it as a way of 'keeping up' with skills and cultural norms. Early days, but I wasn't as enthused about it or about the outcomes as I remember being about learning other programmes.

I guess the answer for now is to keep experimenting, seeing what fits, what takes you somewhere, whether new or old material. That always spells hope.

HOLLY AYLETT BETWEEN TIMES: LIFE ACCORDING TO MY 60S

I have always had the feeling that I've arrived late. I was born in 1955, so too young to really understand '68 and *les evénéments* in Paris as the barricades went up and cobblestones flew across British TV screens. I came too late to university to experience the Garden House riot of 1970 against the Greek junta in Cambridge, or the revolution in the English Department as French structuralists knocked renowned academic F.R. Leavis off his perch, infusing the canons of lit crit with Marxist philosophy. When I bought my speculum and knitting needles and homed in on socialist feminism in conferences around the country, an earlier generation was already unveiling women's experience from motherhood to menopause, rehabilitating wives and lovers long hidden from history. They had mapped out wages for housework and were campaigning for equal rights and the right to control our own bodies. Voices like Sheila Rowbotham and Germaine Greer were revisioning our place in the world. I just followed – little sister.

When I meet someone now, I often try to work out who they were in their 20s, with the sense that for most people, their experiences at that age remain to shape them. Fundamentally, my values have stayed the same since I turned them all inside out in my late teens, then gave the new ones names and spun them into theories at university: an attempt to resolve my deepening conviction that the world was rigged, whatever lens I looked through. The first film I made – documenting the women's struggle in Nicaragua's revolution through the eyes of a rainbow group of feminists from Greenham Common to Brixton Black Sisters – was inspired by my belief that if enough people heard the news, through screenings held from trades' union halls to the House of Commons, we could turn the tide against US imperialism.

I no longer look to national revolution as the inevitable path to change, rather to the constant protests of grassroots resistance, as numerous and varied as the ways power oppresses each human community. I'm mellower perhaps, though no less incensed or resistant to injustice, and I'm as convinced as ever of the power of stories well told to keep us on the right track.

Through learning about my mother's generation, I have understood better how women sit within the promise and restraint of the times they grow up in. In the UK in the 1950s, most were overshadowed by the legacy of war, held in place by the drudgery and dream of homebuilding and an internalised consensus on the role of women that clung like an ill-fitting sweater. My own generation benefited from the reaction that followed, and the sense that it was possible to stand up, proud and outspoken, especially if you came from a background with the privilege not to be silenced.

I marched and demonstrated – Anti-Apartheid, Troops Out, Rock Against Racism, Reclaim the Night, the Miners' Strike. I was a founder member of Broadside, the only all-woman company to take over the editorial of a television current-affairs series, a brief experiment, it turned out, to launch the first year of Channel 4 in 1982. We rejected the notion of 'women's issues', instead affirming women's rights in programmes that showcased stories marginalised by the mainstream – the peace movement, abortion rights, sexism and inequality in the workplace – as well as others that translated news staples such as war or the economy through the voices of the women affected.

Strange to recognise now, in my late 60s and after a long professional life, that I and my contemporaries have been shapeshifters in our different fields. Yet the stepping stones we've laid down need constant defence. As recently as 2016, for the Women's Audiovisual Network, I led a pan-European research exercise into the film industry called 'Where are the Women Directors?': it revealed that of all films released on European screens, only one in five was made by a woman and 84 per cent of funding was invested in productions directed by men. Most shockingly, institutional prejudice also informed national funding bodies, except in Sweden, where the necessity for positive discrimination has been accepted.

Had it been hubris to have thought that we had

made a difference in the 35 years since the start of the 1980s? It was easy to create a moment of shame for the industry – a scud of bad weather to hit the Boulevard de la Croisette at the Cannes Film Festival. But the fact is that Europe's national film institutions had not even been gathering the data, let alone coming up with any change in policy.

Awareness of discrimination heightens your sense of responsibility. I've asked myself to what extent, however unwittingly, I have been the carrier of bias, have helped to perpetuate privilege through assumptions entangled in geopolitics from past decades, if not centuries. In my 20s and 30s, it was the debates in the internationalist solidarity movements that grew my awareness of the impact of colonialism and the slavery underpinning it. This had hardly featured in my school curriculum, and when it did, its impact was disguised through teaching the benefits of Empire for Britain. By keeping it over there, out of sight, history was being sanitised through a syllabus that left us none the wiser.

Most of the first literature on black freedom movements in the UK came from the United States – Toni Cade Bambara, Angela Davis, Toni Morrison – and questions of difference for black communities reached the pages of *Spare Rib* only in the early 1980s. I learned from friends and listened to the outrage of the descendants of slavery. It was for them to forge a language that could free itself from the conceptual frameworks perpetuating racist division.

Before the launch of Channel 4, there were only three broadcast channels for UK audiences, all fed by in-house production and editorial. Channel 4's independent commissioning strategy invited marginalised communities to our screens and effectively made visible what had previously been hidden. Informed by social theorists such as Homi Bhabha and Stuart Hall, films such as *Handsworth Songs* (Black Audio Film Collective) or *The Passion of Remembrance* (Sankofa) revealed the ghosts of songs excluded from the national narrative. I joined *The Bandung File*, a Channel 4 current-affairs series set up and edited by Tariq Ali and Darcus Howe to investigate the missing stories for and about the UK's Asian and Caribbean communities.

We grew stronger by embracing these missing harmonics. Yet almost four decades later, everything seemed out of tune. This time, the perpetuation of white sovereignty was called to account through the Black Lives Matter movement. I re-immersed myself, trying to understand what was being asked of me, how the patterns of my own life could better acknowledge the wounds and debt of slavery, not as historical fact but painfully live. A younger generation was unapologetic and accusatory.

My energies had moved from the picket line through the battle for our screens into the politics of diversity. Tracking terminologies over the years – from multiculturalism to ethnic minorities, to diversity and now cultural diversity – you get a nose for the political game. Shifts in strategy have tended to obscure, if not whitewash, what is actually going on, as well as deflecting any sense of government responsibility. The anglophone response has been pragmatic, targeting the problem through lists and labellings – disability, gender, ethnicity. Targets follow, boxes are ticked – often in exasperation. Though awareness is raised and data is essential, ultimately this culture of diversity officers, reports and departments absolves governments and public institutions. It deflects from the mainstream reform necessary to transform the structural fault lines in our society: poverty, unequal access to good education, class bias and wealth accumulation.

I've gravitated towards concepts of inclusivity and pluralism and within the cultural sector I work to achieve this through the framework of UNESCO's 2005 'Convention on the Protection and Promotion of the Diversity of Cultural Expressions'. Hard fought for by creative workers and with 151 state signatories, its articles aim to advance the security and status of artists, to maximise fair international exchange and to support sustainability through arts practice. Like all United Nations' frameworks, its idealism depends on citizens lobbying to translate best practice into action. I remain hopeful that international solidarity can still upend a world where only one per cent of revenue from cultural goods and services returns to Africa, where giants of the internet spin the globe faster and faster according to their exclusive market logic and where most creative workers just cling on.

Age brings the power of witness – and I'm now sought out by filmmakers who want to know more about how we worked in the 1980s. It wasn't a golden age. Still, our public institutions had not yet succumbed to the pressures of the private sector. Debates about the role played by our public broadcasting space were not yet manipulated down to whether or not the taxpayer could afford a licence fee. The future of our universities was not reduced to a discussion about levels of student fees, concealing the marketisation of learning these fees would usher in. Caught up in the grotesque and serial injustices promulgated by the Tory administrations from 2010, my sense of total alienation flips back to the disasters of the 1980s: how Thatcher's messianic crusade for infinite growth and extraction through globalisation has fed delusions of sovereignty and entitlement in Little England today.

Even though we resisted, I'm part of the generation that now stands accused by the Millennials and Generation Z, who feel their future has been stolen from them. If we were concerned by issues of equality and international development – legacies of the Cold War and shifts in US imperialism – did we question, should we have foreseen, how 'progress' would threaten our very survival? It's profoundly disturbing to realise that we've lost 69 per cent of the planet's wildlife in the past 50 years. Throughout my adult life, I've been presiding over a massacre – as well as the toxification of the food we eat and the air we breathe. Yet it's only in the past decade that I have understood the urgency to act on this.

It's my children's generation and successive cohorts of students I've taught who have kept shifting the fields of my perception. We are part of a human chain and one of the gifts of becoming a mother in my late 30s has been the chance to live alongside two unique beings as they developed: to experience how toddlers absorb and mirror their environment; to witness the vulnerability of jostling clans in teenage years; to remember the juggling of ideals through the impossible clashes of work, lovers and location throughout the turbulent 20s. Most importantly, to be a parent is to try to understand the world through their eyes. Our children are as if on loan: to be delivered into the world they must inherit, to become its next guardians, we must learn how best to release them and hand it on. The world I inherited was shadowed by the threat of extinction through nuclear war. The world I've passed on faces eclipse through the enormity of the climate crisis.

The day that Jean-Paul Sartre died in 1980 I remember vowing to try to grow old like him: to keep curious about the cultures of successive generations, to stay live and to resist nostalgia. This has not been without conflict. While trying to understand the origin and passions of transgender activism, for instance, I have ultimately reasserted rights hard fought for and defended words as fundamental as 'mother' and 'woman'. But the arguments, and the feelings behind them, must out, whether over the felling of a word, a statue or, most recently for me, a 100-year-old plane tree, where engaging with my local community, exposing the issues and politics, has brought discovery and renewal.

I often think of my grandmother, born in candlelight in the Wirral in 1896 in the solid days of Empire. She lived through electrification, votes for women, the replacement of horses with cars then airplanes, and died in an era of sexual liberation and a fragile Commonwealth. That she encountered and survived such an enormous trajectory of change is reassuring as we head for the coming storms of AI. That said, the prospect of fighting off definition by algorithm – invented, let's remember, by a handful of the world's inhabitants, many based in Silicon Valley, almost exclusively male and largely white – is discomforting. Even worse, AI will be accelerated by its own self-defining systems, is being released into a user-generated online environment of consumers not citizens, and no one, it seems, has a clue how to manage this Pandora's Box. The UK government has only just begun on the legacies of Mr Zuckerberg and the dangers of Facebook, launched some 20 years ago.

Amid this acceleration of new technologies, it's worth noting that our planet has been around for about four and a half billion years. If you humanise this impossible figure by projecting it on to an imaginary twelve-hour clock face, nothing comes alive until the hands reach four o'clock. Between four and seven o'clock, only single-cell, squidgy things appear. Homo sapiens arrives just before midnight, in the last tenth of a second of the twelfth hour.

I find this thought comforting: as humbling as losing myself on a walk in the mountains. Nevertheless, however miniscule our significance, this is still our moment. I believe we exist to encourage each other across continents and generations, to nudge each other along, often to shout out loud. What remains ours, after all, is the poetry and music of the present.

ANNA BIRCH

Raising awareness among and about women over 60 is important. For instance, although we have paid our full share of National Insurance contributions, we have been denied our pension rights. Women Against State Pension Inequality (https://www.waspi.co.uk) campaigns to set the record straight. This theft of our pensions by the state is emblematic of the low regard in which women over 60 are held. Inundated by misogynist images in the media since our youth, we now find that capitalism continues its relentless march, negating the value of our life experiences, our ambition, the care we give – and simply put, the lives we live.

Catastrophes and losses, workplace sexual harassment and inequality all impact disproportionally on women. Guilt at not being activist 'enough' in combatting these issues leaves me feeling frustrated and angry.

However, life after 60 has been surprising! Time is becoming more and more valuable. The opportunity to reflect on my life in the hope of gaining a little distance and understanding is important to me. What would my life have been like without having to negotiate the patriarchy and other misogynist political and economic structures?

Right now, shifting stale narratives and asserting a right to a positive collective future is my favourite topic of conversation and action.

ELIZABETH-ANNE WHEAL

For a glorious period starting in the 1970s, women and girls took back authority over their bodies. We said no to being dressed and made-up by men. We said no, too, to the male-conjured myth of women's physical mystery. We stopped hiding from ourselves and we stopped objectifying ourselves. We gave up on squeezing, bleaching, smoothing and sanitising.

Instead, we gifted ourselves permission to get to know and to love our bodies, for themselves. Of all the liberations wrought by the early feminist movement, the freedom to live in, learn about and truly enjoy our bodies – just as they are – was one of the most important, exciting and empowering.

I never expected that for the generations of girls and women following us, that freedom – and that joy – would dwindle away, eclipsed by a combination of toxic millennial masculinity and body-image obsession: by Botox, bum hikes and body contouring; by sexism, body shaming and social media.

I didn't expect selfie woman. I don't recognise her and, more importantly, I worry that she doesn't recognise herself. And if she has been built to pleasure anyone but herself, shouldn't we be reaching out a hand to help her?

CHERRY SMYTH

During the 1980s, I lived a social life of marching. I protested about Troops Out, Reclaim the Night, Section 28, the homophobia preventing treatment for AIDS, and nuclear weapons at Greenham. I'm not sure I expected still to feel the same anger and fervour 40 years on, though I was lucky to meet many older women back then who were publicly protesting about the state of the world, so perhaps I shouldn't be so surprised. I remember clearly a woman in her 60s at the peace camp at Greenham, who'd left her vicar husband and was embracing lesbianism for the first time.

Today, each time I go on a march, especially after being part of the three-million strong, anti-war march that didn't stop the war in Iraq in 2003, I say I'm not doing that again – it's pointless. Yet then, I find the sense of helplessness amid injustice so over-whelming – maybe more so now that I am older – that I simply HAVE to join a march and pick up on that infectious joy and sustaining optimism of protest.

And so, in 2009, I HAD to carry a pair of ghastly black shoes that I'd kept for funerals and throw them over the police cordon towards the Israeli Embassy as a sign of disrespect for Israel's government and sup-port for the Palestinians. I was also aware, as I saw young Muslim men being arrested, that I had a cer-tain safety, being white and middle class and older. It feels wrong to hide behind that privilege.

I still enjoy the energy and slogans of a big march, but recently have been more drawn to the local-scale guerrilla tactics of XR, joining the Schools on Strike for climate emergency on Upper Street in Islington and sitting amid flowers to stop the traffic on Waterloo Bridge in 2019. And how could I be a bystander as the immense wave of protest that is Black Lives Matter swept over the UK? I helped to organise a series of talks about whiteness and how to take more responsibility for it.

I still appreciate the codes and etiquette of solidarity you find in street protests: the truck and bus drivers honking their horns as they pass; the holding up of a banner while someone rests their arm; the sharing of fruit and nuts and stories of how we became agitators. An artist I know says that he paints to 'motivate, activate and move'. That's why I love painting, but it's also why I have retained a deep love of and respect for activism that has not diminished as I age.

JENNY MAYOR
IS THIS WHAT I EXPECTED?

Unlike my mother, I went to university, got involved in left-wing politics and had sexual freedoms. When I had children, mum never understood shared chores and childcare. She loved being a grandmother, though. I watched curiously as she played with my oldest daughter and cuddled the baby in ways I had never known.

Long after she died, it was my turn to read stories to grandchildren snuggled on my lap, pointing at pictures. I pushed them in buggies through streets and parks. My body remembered ways of caring for children as I stroked feverish brows or played silly games. Everyone told me: all the joys without the stress. On feast days I sat at the matriarchal table, feeding my tribe.

In lockdown, a pragmatic choice: bubble with the nearest family, not the one that involved bus rides. This blew open old sibling jealousies, exposing deep fissures. My oldest daughter suddenly declared me a terrible mother and grandmother. Recognising the germ of truth in her words, I recalled the first stumbling months of parenting and mistakes along the way, but it wasn't the whole picture. Rational discussion failed, as did an attempt at family therapy. Like a hurt toddler, she walked away, declaring she wanted an end to all contact with me.

I worked through the agony and grief with a

brilliant counsellor. I talked endlessly to friends and family, shocked by what had happened. Some got angry on my behalf, but I couldn't. Some walked long, therapeutic miles beside me. After a while, there's no more to discuss. We go out and do things and often laugh. When someone talks about their families, I feel an envious ache. I have a loving grandchild and a supportive daughter, who stay close. Also, my daughter's partner and sons. I am mostly cheerful. I've adjusted my life around a great chasm in the middle of it. It's not what I expected.

G.W.

I can't quite recall what I expected life to be like after 60. Now, with both of us in our 70s, our son is living at home with us again. He's an addict and is neuro-divergent. I always thought that this (that everything, in fact!) would get better with time, a naive presumption of an upward direction of travel. But recently it's got worse, with episodes of psychosis that make us fear for his safety. More than once we've come close to having him sectioned, and would have done so, were it not for the support of the Rapid Response and Crisis teams, who were amazing, but who are massively overstretched – and, as their name suggests, leave when the crisis is over. All resources have been cut drastically. If he weren't autistic, we would have 'thrown him out' long ago (in fact we did), but he's too vulnerable at the moment.

This might all sound depressing, but in a strange way it's the making of us. We both still work, which keeps us sane. I'm an artist and writer, and I find the issues that arise from our family dynamic feed my creativity rather than quash it. The discipline of turning up to my tiny messy studio every day is good for me and we are very fortunate to be financially stable. We realise (sort of) that we can't go on like this forever and there is definitely an element of denial, but no talk of downsizing.

CAROLINE WRIGHT

Now in my mid-60s, I continue to feel I am not the woman I thought I was before I reached the age of 50 and experienced the stereotypical menopausal feelings: lack of patience, increased anxiety, mourning my gradual loss of physical strength, being unable to effectively multi-task. Recently I tend to think in terms of how long I have left. I look at my friends, my contemporaries and my beloved older friends and am struck anew by how precious they are and how precious life is.

I have continued to work as an artist with renewed fervour, my mind at times on fire creatively. Work and care responsibilities drop away and I value the time I can spend alone.

Yet new issues have arisen as I experience a deep love for a precious grandchild and watch my adult sons ageing. I am thrilled to witness their lives, lucky to share this time with a loving husband, yet also more deeply anxious about their future and the urgency of saying something meaningful before it's too late.

My deepening anger about the state of our world environmentally and politically contrasts with the wonder of new friends made, new places to live in, and witnessing the beauty of the world. The increased intensity of these responses surprises me.

I have noticed that I have definitely become a less patient woman – micro and macro! I didn't expect life to feel 'more so' not 'less'.

ANNIE CORNBLEET
THE CRACKED WALNUT

The 40s were good – operating with maximum energy, at peak performance. The 50s were horrible – dementia, parents' deaths, over-pressurised work and career. The 60s started so well and then went downhill. I remember how I screamed in the bank, that Thursday morning of my 60th birthday. Those were the days – when teachers received a tax-free lump sum in their bank accounts the moment they turned 60.

Then the reality of retirement kicked in. After a successful and hectic career as a headteacher and arts practitioner for almost 30 years, suddenly I had all the time in the world – and no idea what to do with it. I crashed. Burned out. I felt embarrassed by my good fortune, my privilege – and my inability to deal with it. Others seemed so prepared – they had hobbies and travel plans and grandchildren and were thrilled to move on to this 'next chapter' in their lives.

I felt left out, left behind and pathetic. I watched the clock, amazed at how slowly time passed, at how long each day seemed to last. All those hours and nothing to do.

As a drama teacher, committed to the arts as a vital route into holistic education, especially for disaffected young people, I had written, directed and produced plays throughout my career. After retirement, my interest turned to filmmaking (which unlike a play leaves a permanent legacy) and I embarked on a major project to document my family history and my own life.

But I still had no idea how to define myself. Does writing this make me a writer? Does writing a poem make me a poet? Does making a film make me a film-maker? I don't know. But I did recognise that losing the status of being a headteacher meant I no longer knew who I was or what I wanted.

I realise now that I did not feel I had ever had a voice in my life. Successful career? Tick. Long-term partner? Tick. One grown-up son? Tick. Lots of loving and supportive friends? Tick. But I kept literally losing my voice – a not uncommon problem in the teaching profession, and something I had been plagued with since childhood. Now, as I began to think about how to put my life on screen, the idea of finding and using my voice fully took on a metaphorical meaning.

The film project was completed in time for my 70th birthday, and I planned a big celebration – a coming together of family and friends from near and far, something memorable and significant. But just six days before, my partner had a major stroke – and the walnut of my brain split in two. On the one hand, it was too late to cancel the party, yet on the other my partner was in hospital. A split brain – something from which I'm not sure I've yet fully recovered.

I am now 71 years old and officially designated my partner's Carer. Did I think this is where I would be? No. Is this where I want to be? No. I have entered something like the dark web – a parallel reality I didn't know existed, an underground maze of Social Services, Benefits, GPs and Carers. I struggle to navigate this new world – where all sorts of rights and benefits we are fully entitled to are held back because they don't really want to pay for anyone to have them. It's one thing to understand and sympathise with an NHS and Care System in crisis. But it is another to have to fight so hard for the services we actually need.

I don't want to moan and complain. But I can say that I really don't like what being a Carer has made me feel like. Infinite patience is required and I am a very impatient person. An impossible skill set is needed – incorporating the roles of mother, nurse and partner. Wheelchairs. Attendance Allowance (I was reduced to tears the two times I called their number for help). Physio. Adult Social Care (no one ever answers the phone... and there isn't even a queuing system). There are some very good organisations that really help – Age UK, The Stroke Association, to name but two. But ultimately we are on our own.

I see so many friends who are in pain and suffering. People say, 'What do you expect? It's bound to happen at your age.' But I find myself railing against this. The idea that it could all be so much worse is not helpful to me – rather, it just exacerbates the pain of the situation. And I dread what the future will hold when the rest of my age group, my generation, is faced with needing care – will it be a dystopia where only the fittest survive and the rest of us are swallowed up and spat out?

In the meantime, my main struggle seems to have to do with speed. I buzz about like a neurotic wasp while he remains calm and seemingly quite happy with becoming very, very slow.

So I sing – two choirs, weekly. I lunch with friends, I go to the cinema, I grieve. I plot a new animated short film about becoming a Carer to highlight the fact that though there are voices out there clamouring for change, we are all living so much longer and our infrastructure continues to crumble after so many years of government neglect, mismanagement and underfunding. It makes it difficult to see any chance of positive resolutions within my lifetime.

I recognise that I can't slow down and he can't speed up. But each new day comes, amazingly, and learning to live that day as best I can seems the only way forward. I can't seem to heal the cracked walnut of my brain, but I can try to heal myself a little each and every day.

SALLY SPINKS
MUSINGS ON TURNING 60

I feel that turning 60 this year could be the beginning of something amazing, but there are also questions and conundrums buzzing around my brain.

I'm enjoying a newfound freedom, having scaled down my paid work so I can push my art practice forward, but I'm finding it hard to settle into a routine. Can I find a way to feel as productive as possible with my time, or is this even necessary? Why do I feel guilty about not getting through tasks when there is no deadline or pressure to do so? Surely being an artist is about having the time to muse and reflect? Or is this all part of an underlying feeling that I should be making the most of what time I still have left?

I'm exploring lots of creative openings with my art and I'm making work related both to my mental health and to social injustice. How can I do more with my creativity to galvanise action, for myself and for others? What do I need to do to have more impact? How can I reach a wider audience?

I don't have children and I am both excited and concerned about ageing gracefully, healthily and without being a burden to anyone. If I am left on my own (especially if I live well into my 90s, like most women in my family), how will I organise my old age? How can I use my current network of family and friends to plan the best possible future, whatever the challenges?

It's a lot to figure out, and the starting point, as always, is the questions. But maybe I should be more scared of things I can't predict that might be coming?

For the moment, though, I'm focusing on what I know, using my strong support network of friends to help me to navigate this new world. It's this diversity of perspectives that helps me to explore the options and turn these conundrums into exciting opportunities for this next phase of my life.

NANCY CHARLEY
A SONG OF HIBERNATION

I wrapped my heart in a cotton shroud,
I wound my heart in a silk cocoon,
I gave my heart to the carrion crows
who flew my heart to a lace day moon.

So began a poem I wrote in 2011, approaching 50, moving away from being mother to five children and caring for adults with complex emotional needs. This poem reflected my need to withdraw, readjust, be cocooned. A song of menopause and a changing role.

My heart will return when autumn is dead,
once winter is sifted and spring has sprung,
my heart will stir in its shrouded cocoon,
bloody my body, release my tongue…

Sitting in the garden a couple of weeks ago, the poem came into my mind and set me thinking. Was I still in the cocoon? Have I become full-bloodied? I know I've discovered new loves, have developed old passions and become happier in my skin, more accepting of faults and weaknesses. I've just slipped into the 60+ group this year but I sense a new phase of life is coming so I've set a loose five-year plan to lighten my load, both physically and emotionally. Perhaps the cocoon will crack…

PAULINE BROWN

At 81, I enjoy being invisible: I like not being a sexual object and can be friends with men.

Outside pressures no longer bother me: I can do what I want with my life and I feel liberated.

There is no edge: I can say what I want, talk about anything. I love that.

I am much more comfortable in my head, and able to live more honestly.

I don't care for the infirmity of old age, but otherwise ageing is empowering.

SARAH BAILEY

Once upon a time, the future stretched ahead seemingly endlessly, and striving was the default position. There was much to try to achieve: to own a home, raise children, do a productive job while maintaining family links and friendships. Now, we find ourselves clearing out belongings rather than acquiring them, children are grown, and career potential is disappearing thanks to an ageist work environment.

Also, the inevitable consequence of living longer is that people you love die – and they are doing it more frequently. So how to avoid paralysis and gloom? For me, the answer lies in focusing on the positives age and experience bring.

First, nurture friends, old and new. Age brings decades-old friendships, and life is hugely enriched by them. And never stop making new friends: each one adds something unique and precious.

Second, be brave and try new things. As we grow older, we can become reluctant to put ourselves in situations outside our comfort zone. So try to treat things that make you nervous as adventures and embrace them – even if it's just travelling somewhere where you don't know exactly what lies ahead.

Third, be grateful and look forward. Embrace the joy of a new generation and be kind to anyone you meet. You will have many blessings to count, and you will have the wisdom to know that it is laughter, love and a sense of proportion that are most valuable.

MIDORI NISHIKAWA

I have been suffering from Long Covid since 2021, though I think I am finally coming out of it, albeit slowly. However, my loving family – especially my husband, daughter and granddaughter – have had to watch me deteriorate at an alarming speed over the past two and a half years, from a zippy supergran to a person on crutches. At 71, I feel age is no longer on my side as I recover from ailments so much more slowly. But on the plus side, in taking my time over things, I'm no longer upsetting my own or anyone else's expectations too dramatically.

My parents died when they were in their mid-80s, so I spent my late 50s and early 60s looking after them and dealing with their illnesses, deaths, funerals, taking their ashes back home to Japan, clearing their houses, sorting their wills... It was utterly exhausting.

So I arrived in my mid-60s having been too busy to create much for a while. Having been a painter all my adult life, I have had to change my ideas about how to create, and what to create, learning to redirect my aims and trying to liberate myself from what I had previously thought was achievement.

I have found this truly hard to navigate.

FISH KRISH

The day I turned 60 came and went without any major impact on my psyche, though the surprise party organised by a friend caused me to scream with shock and delight as I found myself confronted by friends and family from across my 60 years.

The last eight years have sped by without my really perceiving a shift, apart from the inevitable invisibility that comes with now being a grey-haired older woman. But I work with young people, who seem generally accepting of me and fairly oblivious to my wrinkles.

At 67, however, I started getting ill at the end of every project I did – projects where I had committed 100 per cent of my energy and was then left exhausted and sick. This new vulnerability was so disorientating, especially as it came with the realisation that I would have to find a way to change gear while still holding on to a sense of myself. This became the new challenge.

I took an unpaid sabbatical for three months, which acted as a brilliant reset. Returning to work, I am trying to break the habit of a lifetime and maintain my passion and commitment without diving in with both feet all the time.

The result is very unsettling as I struggle with my feelings of not being as useful as before, not helped by a young colleague who I suspect thinks that I should be put out to grass. But I am not yet ready to retire and am in fact haunted by the word, which to me signifies both irrelevance and isolation.

So I am struggling in the in-between lands, trying to maintain an interested and flexible mind and to resist others' judgements – and perhaps more significantly, my own preconceptions about ageing.

REBECCA D'MONTÉ

I took early retirement in 2021, having worked as a university lecturer for several decades. It had been planned for three years and I couldn't wait to stop working full-time and take up my lifelong ambition to write (non-academic) books. I have recently completed a cultural memoir about the effects of technology on relationships between men and women and am now starting a psychological thriller. On the surface, I am doing exactly what I set out to do and in this I am fulfilled and happy.

However, what I had not expected was that my health (always precarious) would take a nosedive, particularly in relation to my mobility. Now I find it difficult to walk because of osteoarthritis in my knees and wear and tear in my lower back. This is on top of multiple sclerosis, which I've contended with for years. Because I don't drive, it is difficult to do all the things I'd planned, such as visiting friends across the country, travelling abroad, or even wandering around art galleries and museums. I have moved out of the city (big mistake!) and the health services are scattered across several areas, accessible only by car. (For example, my breast screening check-up was scheduled in a town that was an hour's drive away; nearly two hours by public transport.)

The other problem I hadn't anticipated was loneliness. At the same time that I gave up my job and moved to a different area, my son left home for university. For the first time I was living on my own, and while I like my own company, the silence was deafening. I have built up a social life of sorts and now have a writing group, a book club and art classes I attend, and a few other friends outside of this as well. However, I can easily go for five days or more without seeing anyone, which is why I spend a lot of time frequenting cafés so that at least there is some kind of human contact.

I am told that I look a lot younger than people of my own age (66) and when I've attended activities run by U3A, etc., I feel quite out of place. Society seems to be running behind how recently retired professional women view themselves: the mindset is still that of an older generation brought up during the Second World War, rather than women who grew up during Second Wave Feminism and in the Glam Rock and Punk Rock eras.

KAREN WADE

Stuck in one of those long marriages – not good enough to stay for, not bad enough to leave – I was lacklustre and out of shape. As each child left home, another part of me faded away.

Rowing changed all this – low impact, increased flexibility and strength, accompanied by camaraderie second to none. I was a late starter with no previous experience, but it taught me to stop lying about my age and to start being proud of it.

Since then, I have met other women rowers worldwide, in their 60s and beyond – all pioneers, living longer than previous generations, with no template to follow. All growing fitter, more visible, more vital. All grateful for that *Sliding Doors* moment of discovering the joy of rowing their way through later life. All painfully aware of how our alternative life without rowing might have been.

I'm (probably) not going to set any records. I have no illusions; nothing to prove. I have set myself a little venture though: to row under the bridges of the world. At 65, I don't need to run with the wolves any more. I can saunter with attitude, with women just like me.

I think Young Me would like this Older Me. And I like her too.

POL MARSON

One New Year's Eve I heard that the reason people tend not to keep their resolutions is because they think in big units of time, for instance, 'Next year I'll give up smoking', giving themselves the whole year never to get around to it. The suggested solution was that you should try to create smaller, more urgent timeframes. I was intrigued and tried to calculate how many days I might still have to live: 350 x 20 = 7000 (I couldn't do 365 days x 20 years in my head). I have found this very motivating: I hardly waste a day!

The other thing I find helpful is dance. I was given a ballroom-dancing lesson for my 50th birthday and ended up competing until about five years ago (I'm now 70 years old). Then I found a contemporary dance class online during lockdown and I'm now having the time of my life as part of a group of over-60s dancers.

ANN TRENEMAN THE EMPTY HOUSE

A few months after my husband Ian died just under a year ago, someone said to me: 'But surely you knew that he would go first?'

Hmmm, I thought, this makes a change from the usual condolences. 'No,' I said. 'I didn't.'

'You must have. He was seven years older,' said my friend.

But I didn't know or, if I did, I figured in some vague way that he would die before me, but some time further in the future. Much further. As in over the horizon. Not when he did, on the first day of February, when he was 74 and I was 66, newly semi-retired, with my long list of things we could do together now I wasn't so busy all the time. Wait, I wanted to say, as death chose our door to visit out of all the doors on the street. Can we have just a little more time to do all the things we would have done? Please. But I now know that bargaining is one of the stages of grief.

I have been a people-watcher all my life and, since I was young, I have looked at older couples walking along a road, or in a shop, and been moved by what I see. The guiding hand on the elbow. The exchange of words as they look in a shop window together. The way you can get a flash, sometimes, of a younger face. The almost choreographed way they move together around a supermarket, familiar with their roles, one choosing items from a shelf, the other beetling off to find something else. They click along, tick tick tock, like clockwork, after a lifetime of shared moments. It is a snapshot, a Polaroid instant: a couple who have lived through it all and come out the other side, still walking along together, still interested in what each other is saying.

It is a sight that, at times, can bring tears, quick and quiet, and I have realised there must be a yearning inside me for this. My father died in his 40s and so I never saw my parents as oldsters together. My grandparents lived far away. Companionship, slippery as a bar of soap, has never come easily. In so many ways, it has been natural to be an outsider. If you live in an adopted country, as I do (I was born and lived in America until I was 28), then you can't help but see it through a stranger's eye. If you work as a writer, as I have all my life, then you are as much an observer as a participant. Looking back, I'm not surprised that my own first attempt at companionship ended in divorce in my mid-30s.

At age 48, I sat back and took stock. My children were more or less launched into the world. My job had ceased to be all-consuming. I didn't want to be that woman who worked until she dropped and had only colleagues at her funeral. Nor did I fancy growing old like Jenny Joseph's proverbial woman, 'wearing purple' and generally being outrageous. I'd already worn enough purple, I felt. I wasn't so much lonely as tired of being alone. I felt that tug that I imagine most people experience at a much younger age. I wanted to find someone to walk down the street with me as we both grew older.

I met Ian when I was 50 at what was, after two years of online dating, my tried-and-tested first-date formula of Saturday lunch at Pizza Express. This made it easy to escape if it was all too boring. In our case, after my Salade Niçoise and his Pizza Americano, we ended up going for a walk in the local park. It's always a good sign when it starts to drizzle and neither of you mentions it because you don't want the walk to end. We had shared interests – hiking, music and politics – and got along well. I soon realised that almost all the rulebooks are geared towards the young. When you are older, you find your own way to negotiate the whitewater rapids that is any relationship (at least the ones that I've had).

What made Ian's death, quick and brutal, even more infuriating was that we'd chosen each other specifically because we wanted to grow old with someone. We'd both been single for ages and had arrived at the same point, though living in different places and unknown to each other, where we were tired of the same old, same old. We had no shared history, neither children nor city nor friends, so we made our own over the next 16 years: we moved to Derbyshire, bought a home, walked the hills and got used to life together.

We would never know how long Ian had been ill, at which point exactly the cancer decided to take up residence in his lung, then move to his brain. It was just six weeks from the day we were told in Chesterfield hospital's A&E department that he had a tumour to the midwinter morning when he died at home. It was an immensely intense period of togetherness: we had never been so vital to each other. I was the living memory, the helper, the enabler. He was the patient, the one in danger, the one desperate to live. I found life as a carer exhausting but also fulfilling in a strange way. 'You didn't sign up for this,' he told me one day as we maneuvered, with great difficulty, up a set of stairs. Yes, I did, I thought. This is what being a companion is all about.

Our world grew smaller in ever decreasing circles. We went for drives or out for coffee. One day he had a haircut and it seemed such a triumph. Then leaving the house became too hard, so the goal would be to walk this distance, or go up the stairs, or eat this dessert. We were convinced that he would get well enough to start treatment. Then one day, out of the blue, a series of words came into my brain. At first, it was more of a rhythm, a bit like a horse's canter, that wouldn't go away. Gradually, I absent-mindedly began to try to put words to it. I thought it was a lyric from a song but then certain words surfaced and I realised it was from a poem. But which? I found the answer in a book by Emily Dickinson:

> Because I could not stop for Death –
> He kindly stopped for me –
> The Carriage held but just Ourselves –
> And Immortality.

I sat in the front room, by myself, reading those words and I knew – absolutely knew, in my heart – that Ian was going to die soon. Death was going to stop for him. The carriage was already on its way. I took in this information, guarding it, and told no one.

Those last weeks were a strange mixture of extreme closeness and something I now think of as 'pre-grieving'. I ran through all the things we would never do again – never go back to Paris, spend time in London, return to the Isle of Skye, do our favourite walk around Semerwater in Wensleydale. Never go to the movies, to a concert, argue about politics, decide that this was a night to go out because we both hate take-aways. So many things flitted through my mind. We would never catch each other's eye at a party, put up Christmas lights, fail to agree on the way to cook a chicken.

When Death did stop, I was still surprised at his speed. For me, most markedly, from the very first day, the aftermath has been pervaded by the eerie sense of hollowness inside our home. For months, it was hard to come back to the house for, as I entered the door, I would realise all over again that no one was there but me. As the months rolled by, I often no longer missed Ian specifically but almost always felt that something intangible was missing. Even as I write this, I know that I will stop at some point and wonder, for just a nano-second, if I need to tell Ian I'm going for a walk. It was only now that I truly understood what another widow told me about how she felt when her partner died. Outside the home, she said, life is not so different from before. But when you walk back into the house, through that door, your life is completely different. There's only you. You mourn not just a person, but a way of life, a shared mentality, a daily companionship.

The question asked in this phase of the Ida Project was: 'Is this what we expected?' Although I have, in the past, prided myself on often being able to see and play the long game, my answer has to be, most definitely, no. For me, being over 60 was to be a period when I would go on discovering a world beyond my career and my children. It was to be about having time to do all those things on my list now I was not so preoccupied by work. It was to be about learning how to grow old gracefully or, sometimes perhaps, disgracefully. And I had taken the liberty of thinking I would do all those things as part of one of those couples walking down the street, the arthritis slowing our pace, as we chatted or looked in a window.

I increasingly find that, whatever I am looking for, be it an item or an idea, it is something that I already have, tucked away in a cupboard or a file or a compartment of my brain. In this whole extraordinary period, the thing that I had forgotten was something I had known all along. I had allowed myself to ignore the fact that life can change in an instant. A click of the fingers. A door shutting. One sentence as short as 'there is a tumour'. So often, everyday living trundles along, sometimes for ages, pretty much as expected. But one day, it won't. It will change. This is something to remember at any age, but in particular, for me, now. In answer to my friend's question about knowing that Ian would die before me, I would now say: 'Yes, I must have known. I just didn't pay any attention.'

BIBI BROWN

Recently, I turned 80. I had a big party at a barn near Waterloo, with a seven-piece Afro-beat band and a mix of friends and family, young and old. One of my nephews said it was like being at Glastonbury.

So now I am on the other side – heading to the big 90. I am well, AND I have a heart condition. The medics call it heart failure, but I protested: my heart hasn't failed. It is still working – just not working as well as it did. It skips beats and the lower atrial chamber is slightly distended, so I run out of puff, especially walking up stairs or inclines. I get tired, and the beta-blocker I take daily interferes with the clarity of my dreams (I really resent this!). Oh well. I take the drugs – along with blood thinners and various supplements – and that's it.

So... now to the heart that has not failed, the heart at the centre of all things. And I find that this heart amplifies and blossoms, the older I get. It is robust and unstoppable and will wing its way with me into the next dimension when this adventure has ceased and the physical heart is laid to rest.

EILEEN CAMPBELL THE SPIRITUAL PATH

Now in my mid-70s, I have travelled the world, but I find that the outer journeys, exciting as they have been, do not match up to the inner one.

As my body becomes slower with osteoarthritis and I have more frequent memory lapses, the inner journey, the spiritual path, brings greater rewards and contentment. I've discovered that ageing can be enriching as I'm more inclined to self-reflection and just being in the moment, not something my younger self could have imagined.

In my youth, as a seeker for answers to life's essential questions, I enthusiastically embraced this or that institutional religion, believing I would find the truth if I followed the practices prescribed by spiritual teachers and gurus. Many of these practices – yoga, meditation, prayer, chanting, visualisation, affirmations – have been of great value to me through life's inevitable ups and downs, and I am grateful to have been pointed in a direction that remains beneficial.

I have not discovered such a thing as 'the truth', only that the answers for each of us are to be found within. A finger can point the way, but only the individual can make a choice appropriate to her development. So allow the path to unfold before you, follow your heart and remain true to your unfolding and authentic self. Even 'mistakes' or 'wrong choices' reveal something we need to know in our personal evolution.

All we ever are is a channel for the life-force to flow through us. The more open and free from prejudices and brain-washing we become, the greater the good we can do. When we reach a point in our understanding where no effort is required to be kind to one another, where this is simply the expression of how we feel about the richness of existence and an overwhelming sense of gratitude, this is the greatest thing we can learn. And sharing with others this understanding of who we are and what we are fortunate enough to enjoy in our lives is real communion.

BELINDA BUDGE
A SHORT NOTE ON MY PROCESS

'If you don't become speechless when looking out into space on a clear night, you are not really looking, and not aware of the totality of what is.'
Eckhart Tolle, *A New Earth: Awakening to Your Life's Purpose*

I couldn't remember the last time I took a moment to look up at the moon and stars. I couldn't remember the last time I experienced that moment of stillness and awe as I gazed at the vastness of the night sky.

I lived in the city, its fast and hurried energy often assaulting my senses, upsetting my equilibrium. My only purpose was to achieve. I had slipped into default mode, drifting through cycle after cycle of my beloved job.

As I headed towards my 60s, my motivation for change was to live in the present moment and to pay attention. Not to live in the anxiety of the past or of the future.

I was looking for a cocoon, some protection and containment from the outside world. So I retreated to a secret safe place, a house surrounded by fields, sheltered and protected – somewhere I could take my time and take stock.

It was a place from which I could look outwards as well as inwards, to come to an understanding of what might be my purpose – a place of stillness from which I could re-emerge into the adventure of what I hoped would be the last third of my life.

Now in my mid-60s, I have found a different way to be in the world, to engage where I can make an impact, effect a change, start a conversation. And to pay close attention to purpose through creativity, traversing familiar paths through the chalk and walnut layers of my landscape, making new patterns.

I pay attention to what captures me. To what takes me beyond. And to the vastness of the night sky.

SUE BLUNDELL CARPE DIEM

Selene, goddess of the moon, fell in love with a beautiful young shepherd called Endymion. She begged Zeus, ruler of the gods, to make him immortal, and also to put him to sleep so that he wouldn't ever age. Every evening she got up to gaze at him.

So the Greeks realised that eternal life meant eternal ageing, and warned us not to wish for it. Sleeping through the day isn't the answer: who would want to live forever if it meant being in a coma?

I too am trying to come to terms with my mortality. But it's making me rather anxious, because there's still so much I need to do before I go. Last year I was just happy to have survived the Covid pandemic. This year I've been back at work, inventing new projects for myself. They are legion.

'Carpe diem,' as the Roman poet Horace memorably advised us (*Odes* 1.11). After all, you never do know when your end is coming:

While we speak, envious time is fleeing: so
     pluck the day,
And believe in the future as little as possible.

Now that I'm 76, I'm doing my best to follow this sensible advice. As a result, my life seems to be much the same as it was when I was 20. I'm still worrying about time, and about my to-do list. Hopefully this will at least help to keep me young – just like Endymion, but without the coma.

GERRIE TER HAAR

I am a woman well beyond the age of 60. In fact, I am 77 years old at the time of writing, and I expect to live on for at least another ten years. If not, I will neither be surprised nor feel betrayed in my expectations. Life has taught me that the best things happen unexpectedly. The worst things too, such as the unexpected death of loved ones.

My life has been full of surprises, both positive and negative, personally as well as professionally. One of the greatest surprises has been that even negative experiences can turn positive. Philosophical reflection and literary imagination are great tools to help us to see this. Or, as one Dutch-Iranian writer phrased it, perhaps we have to die first to see the wonders of life. Such is the creative power of the imagination.

When we were born, none of us expected life, but all of us expect death, one day. Embracing life as I found it, or – better – as it found me, has brought me wonders far beyond my expectation and made me into who I am today. I can't wait to see what life still holds in store for me.

Thank you again to everyone who has
engaged with The Ida Project.

If you would like to order one or more
copies of this book, or join in with the
conversation, please email us at:
info@theidaproject.com

First published in 2023 for
The Ida Project
info@theidaproject.com
by Categorical Books, 73 Tower Road South,
Bristol BS30 8BW

ISBN 978-1-904662-26-6
A CIP record for this book is available from
the British Library

Printed in the UK by Dayfold Group